Celebrations in My World

# Halloween

Molly
Aloian

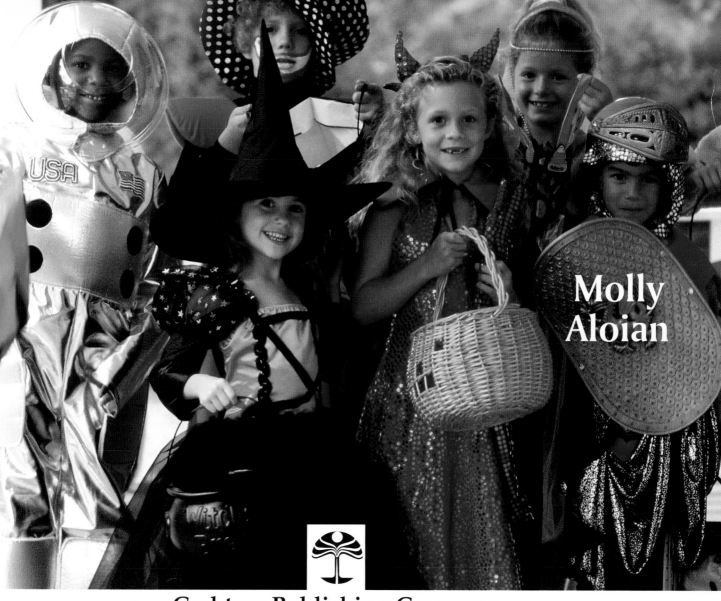

Crabtree Publishing Company
www.crabtreebooks.com

# Crabtree Publishing Company

## www.crabtreebooks.com

**Author:** Molly Aloian
**Coordinating editor:** Chester Fisher
**Series and project editor:** Penny Dowdy
**Editor:** Adrianna Morganelli
**Proofreader:** Crystal Sikkens
**Project editor:** Robert Walker
**Production coordinator:** Katherine Berti
**Prepress technician:** Katherine Berti
**Project manager:** Kumar Kunal (Q2AMEDIA)
**Art direction:** Dibakar Acharjee (Q2AMEDIA)
**Cover design:** Tarang Saggar (Q2AMEDIA)
**Design:** Ritu Chopra (Q2AMEDIA)
**Photo research:** Farheen Aadil (Q2AMEDIA)

**Photographs:**
Alamy: Jim Corwin: p. 15; David Gowans: p. 4; David Grossman: p. 27; Tim Hill: p. 26; D. Hurst: p. 23; Imagebroker : p. 19; Don Mason: p. 9; David L. Moore: p. 25; The National Trust Photolibrary: p. 29; picturesbyrob: p. 14; Peter Steiner: p. 10; Peter Titmuss: p. 5; Nik Wheeler: p. 8
BigStockPhoto: Borce Gjorgjievski: p. 6; Zoran Jagrovic: p. 7
Corbis: Ariel Skelley: p. 1, 12
Dreamstime.com: Mcininch: front cover (children with pumpkins)
Gettyimages: Trish Lease/Stringer: p. 24; Scott Stulberg: p. 30
Istockphoto: Jani Bryson Studios: p. 17
Jupiterimages: p. 16, 21; Comstock Images: p. 13; DreamPictures/VStock: p. 22; Image Source: p. 18; Liquidlibrary: p. 31
Shutterstock: Gary L. Brewer: front cover (background); Sebastian Kaulitzki: folio glyph; Sparkling Moments Photography: p. 11; Monkey Business Images: p. 28; James Thew: front cover (bottom right); Lisa F. Young: p. 20

Library and Archives Canada Cataloguing in Publication

Aloian, Molly
       Halloween / Molly Aloian.

(Celebrations in my world)
Includes index.
ISBN 978-0-7787-4292-0 (bound).--ISBN 978-0-7787-4310-1 (pbk.)

       1. Halloween--Juvenile literature.
I. Title.  II. Series: Celebrations in my world

GT4965.A46 2009          j394.2646          C2009-900231-0

Library of Congress Cataloging-in-Publication Data

Aloian, Molly.
   Halloween / Molly Aloian.
       p. cm. -- (Celebrations in my world)
   Includes index.
   ISBN 978-0-7787-4310-1 (pbk. : alk. paper) -- ISBN 978-0-7787-4292-0
(reinforced library binding : alk. paper)
   1. Halloween--Juvenile literature.  I. Title. II. Series.

GT4965.A432 2009
394.2646--dc22
                                                          2009000327

## Crabtree Publishing Company

**Published in Canada**
**Crabtree Publishing**
616 Welland Ave.
St. Catharines, ON
L2M 5V6

**Published in the United States**
**Crabtree Publishing**
PMB16A
350 Fifth Ave., Suite 3308
New York, NY  10118

**Published in the United Kingdom**
**Crabtree Publishing**
White Cross Mills
High Town, Lancaster
LA1 4XS

**Published in Australia**
**Crabtree Publishing**
386 Mt. Alexander Rd.
Ascot Vale (Melbourne)
VIC 3032

# Contents

What is Halloween? .................. 4

Scaring Spirits Away ................. 6

All Saints' Day ..................... 8

Harvest Time! ...................... 10

Pumpkins ......................... 12

Other Decorations ................. 14

Dressing Up ....................... 16

Halloween Day .................... 18

Trick-or-Treat! ..................... 20

Staying Safe ...................... 22

UNICEF .......................... 24

Halloween Parties ................. 26

Bobbing for Apples ............... 28

Halloween Stories ................. 30

Glossary and Index ............... 32

# What is Halloween?

Halloween is a holiday. People celebrate Halloween on October 31 each year. They dress up in costumes and participate in different activities. People celebrate Halloween in countries all over the world, including Japan, the United Kingdom, and Ireland.

- Halloween takes place during autumn when crops such as pumpkins and hay are ready to pick.

DID YOU KNOW?

*Halloween is one of the world's oldest holidays. People have been celebrating it for hundreds of years.*

People dress up in costumes to celebrate Halloween.

Halloween is an **ancient**, or very old, holiday. It is important to honor **traditions** from the past.

# Scaring Spirits Away

Halloween comes from the ancient **Celtic** holiday called Samhain. Celtic people lived in England, Scotland, and Ireland. Samhain took place around October 31 each year. Long ago, Celtic people believed that the spirits of people who had died rose and caused trouble during Samhain.

The light from a **bonfire** helped to guide spirits to the next world.

People lit huge bonfires and wore costumes to calm the spirits down or scare them away.

During Samhain, people honored the souls of those who had died in the past year.

# All Saints' Day

The Catholic Church has been celebrating All Saints' Day for hundreds of years. All Saints' Day is also called All Hallows' Day. The word hallow means "saint" in Old English. October 31, the night before All Hallows' Day, was called All Hallows' Eve. It was shortened to Halloween.

● These people are at a cemetery in Mexico. They are celebrating All Saint's Day.

DID YOU KNOW?

*On November 2, Christians celebrate All Souls' Day. On this day, they pray for the souls of their dead friends and relatives.*

This girl is celebrating Halloween in Japan.

Celtic traditions and the ideas from the Catholic Church combined. People began wearing costumes and eating special foods to celebrate Halloween.

9

# Harvest Time!

Roman traditions from **harvest** festivals also became part of Halloween. People celebrated their harvests of corn, apples, and other foods in autumn. A Roman autumn festival was called Cerelia. It honored Ceres, the goddess of crops, such as grains. This is why these foods are used at Halloween.

These children are on a ride through a pumpkin patch.

## DID YOU KNOW?

*Long ago, ancient Roman people held a festival called Feralia. They honored the dead during this time.*

Today, people drink apple cider, roast pumpkin seeds, and go apple-picking to celebrate Halloween. Others take hay rides through grain fields.

This boy is looking for the perfect apple to pick.

# Pumpkins

Pumpkins are the most famous **symbols** of Halloween. People carve pumpkins into jack-o'-lanterns. The jack-o'-lanterns are Halloween decorations. Irish and Scottish people once used **turnips** as jack-o'-lanterns. In the 1800s, some people moved to the United States and Canada. They began using pumpkins for jack-o'-lanterns instead of turnips.

These children are searching for the perfect Halloween pumpkin.

DID YOU KNOW?

*Halloween night is called Pooky Night in some parts of Ireland.*

You must be very careful when you are carving a pumpkin. Ask an adult to help you.

Today, many people visit pumpkin patches as part of their Halloween celebrations.

13

# Other Decorations

There are many other spooky Halloween decorations. People decorate with ghosts, skeletons, spiders, and cobwebs. Witches, monsters, candles, and black cats appear in windows of homes and in their yards.

This family decorated their front yard for Halloween.

DID YOU KNOW?

*Some neighborhoods have contests to see who can decorate for Halloween the best!*

Owls, bats, and vampires also make good Halloween decorations. People decorate homes, schools, offices, and public parks. Sometimes, people prepare for weeks to get ready for Halloween.

This front porch is decorated with carved pumpkins for Halloween.

# Dressing Up

People celebrate Halloween by dressing up in costumes. Everyone plans what he or she will wear on Halloween night. Some people buy their costumes. Other people make their costumes. Some people even dress up their pets!

● This girl's mother is helping her with her mouse costume.

## DID YOU KNOW?

*Children's Halloween costumes from the 1950s and 1960s are now worth hundreds of dollars!*

It is fun to see your friends dressed up in their Halloween costumes.

You do not have to dress as something scary on Halloween. You can wear any costume you like! Ask an adult to help you think of an imaginative or fun costume.

17

# Halloween Day

If Halloween is on a school day, you may get to go to school in your costume. It is fun seeing all your classmates and teachers dressed in costumes.

This boy has won first prize in a Halloween contest.

## DID YOU KNOW?

*In some cities, such as Tokyo, Japan, people march in Halloween parades on Halloween day.*

18

This girl is performing a Halloween play at school.

At school, children sing Halloween songs, play games, put on plays, and have parties to celebrate Halloween. Some schools have contests for the best costume. The person with the scariest or most **creative** Halloween costume gets a prize.

19

# Trick-or-Treat!

Trick-or-treating is one of the best parts of Halloween. Children knock on doors and ask "Trick-or-treat?" People give the children candy or other treats.

Someone is giving these kids their treats!

## DID YOU KNOW?

*Children may trick-or-treat for a few hours. Some kids come home with enough candy and treats to fill a pillowcase!*

Trick-or-treating
is a lot of fun.

What is the "trick?" People used to play
**harmless** pranks if they did not get a treat.

Trick-or-treating began long ago in
Europe. Poor people went door to door
on All Saints' Day. They begged for food.
In return, the beggars promised that they
would pray for the family's dead relatives.

21

# Staying Safe

This girl is sorting through her candy with an adult.

Safety must come first on Halloween. You should plan your trick-or-treating route ahead of time. It is important to always go trick-or-treating with an adult.

DID YOU KNOW?

You should only trick-or-treat in well-lit neighborhoods that you know.

Bring a flashlight and try to wear a costume with bright colors so people can see you in the dark. Do not wear masks that make it hard to see. You may not be able to see moving cars. Do not eat any treats until you get home. An adult should look through all of your candy to be sure it is safe.

A flashlight will help this boy see his way in the dark on Halloween night.

# UNICEF

Many children trick-or-treat for UNICEF. Children around the world get food, clean water, education, and medicine from UNICEF.

Each Halloween, people donate millions of dollars to UNICEF.

## DID YOU KNOW?

*A campaign called Trick-or-Treat for UNICEF is the most popular **fundraising** activity throughout Canada.*

These UNICEF boxes are used for collecting money.

Trick-or-treaters carry special UNICEF boxes. They ask friends and neighbors to give money instead of candy.

The day after Halloween, children bring the boxes into school. The teachers send all the money to UNICEF.

# Halloween Parties

Some people hold Halloween parties for their families and friends. People tell stories and play games at Halloween parties. Other people visit haunted houses at carnivals or fairs in their neighborhoods.

● Pumpkin soup is a delicious food to serve at a Halloween party.

DID YOU KNOW?

*People decorate their party foods as ghosts, witches, and other scary things.*

People eat special foods at Halloween parties, including pumpkin seeds and creamy pumpkin soup. They play CDs with eerie sounds. This sets the mood at their parties. The scary music is the perfect background for telling ghost stories!

These people are celebrating at a Halloween party.

# Bobbing for Apples

At some Halloween parties, people bob for apples. They use their teeth to grab an apple that is floating in a tub of water. They are not allowed to use their hands.

● This boy is bobbing for apples with his hands behind his back.

DID YOU KNOW?

*Apples are not as dense as water so they will float in a tub or bucket of water.*

In Roman times, Pomona was the goddess of fruit and trees. The apple was her symbol. Bobbing for apples is one of the oldest and most traditional Halloween games.

This picture shows the goddess Pomona.

# Halloween Stories

There are many well-known Halloween stories. *The Legend of Sleepy Hollow* and *The Great Pumpkin* are stories that people enjoy around Halloween. Some people even make up their own Halloween stories!

This boy is reading a Halloween story.

## DID YOU KNOW?

The Legend of Sleepy Hollow *is a story that features a character known as the headless horseman.*

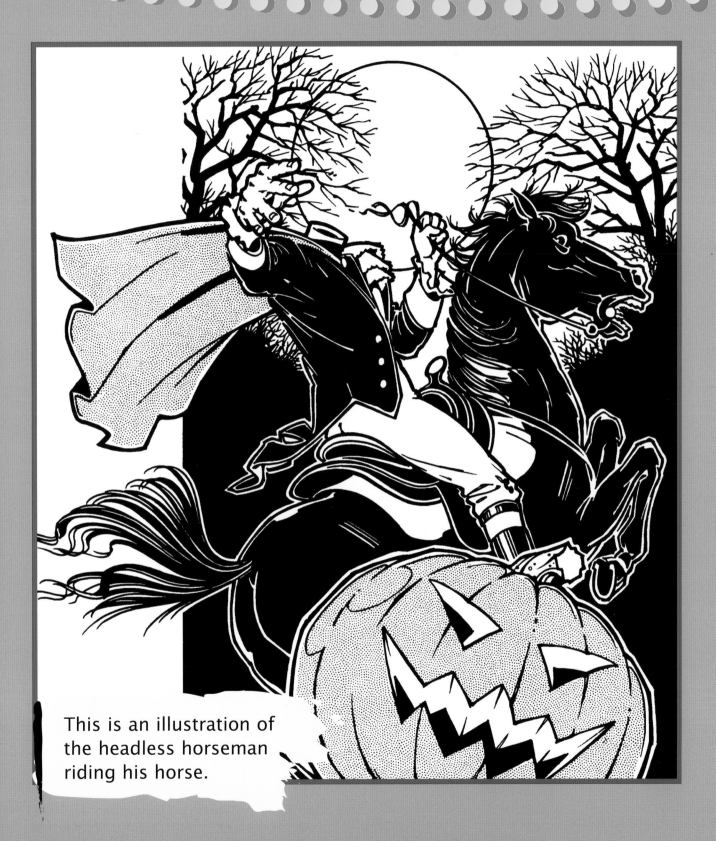

This is an illustration of the headless horseman riding his horse.

Visit your local library or movie store to find a scary book or movie.

# Glossary

**ancient** Something that is very old

**bonfire** A large outdoor fire made with stacked logs

**Celtic** Relating to the Celts or their languages

**creative** Something new and original

**fundraising** Raising money for a cause

**harmless** Unable to harm

**harvest** The picking or collection of ripe fruit, vegetables, or grain

**symbol** Something that stands for something else

**tradition** Information, beliefs, or customs handed down from one generation to another

**turnip** An herb with thick, edible roots

# Index

apples 10, 11, 28, 29

All Saints' Day 8, 9, 21

bonfires 6, 7

costumes 4, 5, 7, 9, 16, 17, 18, 19, 23

decorations 12, 14, 15, 26

foods 9, 10, 21, 24, 26, 27

games 11, 19, 26, 29

Ireland 4, 6, 12

jack-o'-lanterns 12, 13

Japan 4, 9, 18

parades 18

parties 19, 26–27, 28

pumpkins 4, 10, 11, 12, 13, 15, 26, 27

Romans 10, 29

safety 22–23

Samhain 6, 7

school 18, 19, 25

songs 19

spirits 6, 7

stories 26, 27, 30–31

traditions 5, 9, 10

treats 20, 21, 22, 23, 25

trick-or-treating 20, 21, 22, 24, 25

UNICEF 24, 25

Printed in the U.S.A. - CG